THIS PLANNER BELONGS TO:

_____

_____

Dedication

This Project Planner Journal Log is dedicated to all the hard workers out there who love planning out their projects and want to document their findings in the process.

You are my inspiration for producing books and I'm honored to be a part of keeping all of your project planning notes and records organized.

This journal notebook will help you record your details about your project.

Thoughtfully put together with these sections to record:

Project Planner & Goals, Work Hours Log, Project Progress, Tasks List, Productivity Wheel, Schedule, Time Tracker & much more!

How to Use this Book

The purpose of this book is to keep all of your Project notes all in one place. It will help keep you organized.

This Project Planner Journal will allow you to accurately document every detail about your project. It's a great way to chart your course through seeing your project through successfully.

Here are examples of the prompts for you to fill in and write about your experience in this book:

1. **Monthly Planner & Goals Page** - List your goals & top priorities for the month.

2. **Project Planner & Goals** - List your project name, start date, deadline, information & action plan, tools & resources. Project to do list, ideas, concepts & action plan overview.

3. **Work Hours Log** - Task details, date & hours worked.

4. **Project Progress** - Track your progress.

5. **Project Tasks List** - Action steps for tasks, due date & tick box for completion.

6. **Productivity Planner** - Daily goals & priorities, main task, secondary task, other tasks.

7. **Weekly Planner** - Weekly overview of your tasks planned plus notes section.

8. **Productivity Wheel** - Color chart to track productivity.

9. **Weekly Schedule** - Hour by hour for the weekly schedule.

10. **Project Time Tracker** - 15-minute tracker to check as completed.

11. **Project Manager** - 5-week goal tracker.

12. **Month In Review** - Summarize your month with reflection, highlights, improve & focus.

13. **Daily Goal Tracker** - Track the progress of your goals.

14. **Daily Schedule & Priorities** - Hour by hour schedule, reminders, today's to-do list, notes.

My Monthly PLANNER

MONTH:

**TOP
PRIORITY**

TOP GOALS

MONDAY	TUESDAY	WEDNESDAY	THURSDAY	FRIDAY	SATURDAY	SUNDAY

NOTES:

My MONTHLY PLAN

THE MONTH OF

TOP 3 TASKS

MOST IMPORTANT TASKS

NOTES & SCRIBBLES

SUNDAY	MONDAY	TUESDAY	WEDNESDAY	THURSDAY	FRIDAY	SATURDAY

PROJECT PLANNER

Project Information & Action Plan

Project:

Start Date:

Deadline:

To Do

Notes & Reminders

Completed To Do List?

Note:

my PROJECT PLANNER

MY PROJECT GOALS   MY GOAL   ACTION PLAN   DUE ✓

START

DUE

TOOLS & RESOURCES

NOTES & DOODLES

my WORK HOURS LOG

TASK DETAILS   DATE   HOURS

TOTAL HOURS

my PROJECT PROGRESS

PROJECT ONE

| Goal | Start Date | Due Date |

PROJECT TWO

| Goal | Start Date | Due Date |

PROJECT THREE

| Goal | Start Date | Due Date |

PROJECT FOUR

| Goal | Start Date | Due Date |

PROJECT FIVE

| Goal | Start Date | Due Date |

PROJECT NAME:

ACTION STEPS / TASKS   DUE   ✓

my DAILY PRODUCTIVITY PLANNER

TODAY'S DATE

THE MAIN TASK

Daily Goals & Priorities

Start   Finish

SECONDARY TASKS

Notes & Reminders

1.

TODAY'S SCHEDULE

Start   Finish

2.

Daily Overview

Start   Finish

3.

Start   Finish

OTHER TASKS

NOTES & SCRIBBLES

1.

Start   Finish

2.

Start   Finish

3.

Start   Finish

my WEEKLY PLAN

MONDAY

TUESDAY

WEDNESDAY

THURSDAY

FRIDAY

SATURDAY

SUNDAY

THE WEEK OF

TOP THREE TASKS

1.

2.

3.

OTHER TASKS

MY NOTES

PROJECT PLANNER

PROJECT TITLE: BUDGET:

START DATE: DUE DATE: DURATION: COMPLETED:

PROJECT TO DO LIST   IDEAS * DOODLES * CONCEPTS * NOTES

                                                    ACTION PLAN OVERVIEW

NOTES

my PRODUCTIVITY WHEEL

Jot down your daily activities, goals and priorities on the spaces below. Assign every activity a unique color by filling in the circle that corresponds with it. Color in each hour of the day based on which activity you have completed.

Are you utilizing your time effectively? Are you reaching goals and focusing your time on your most important priorities?

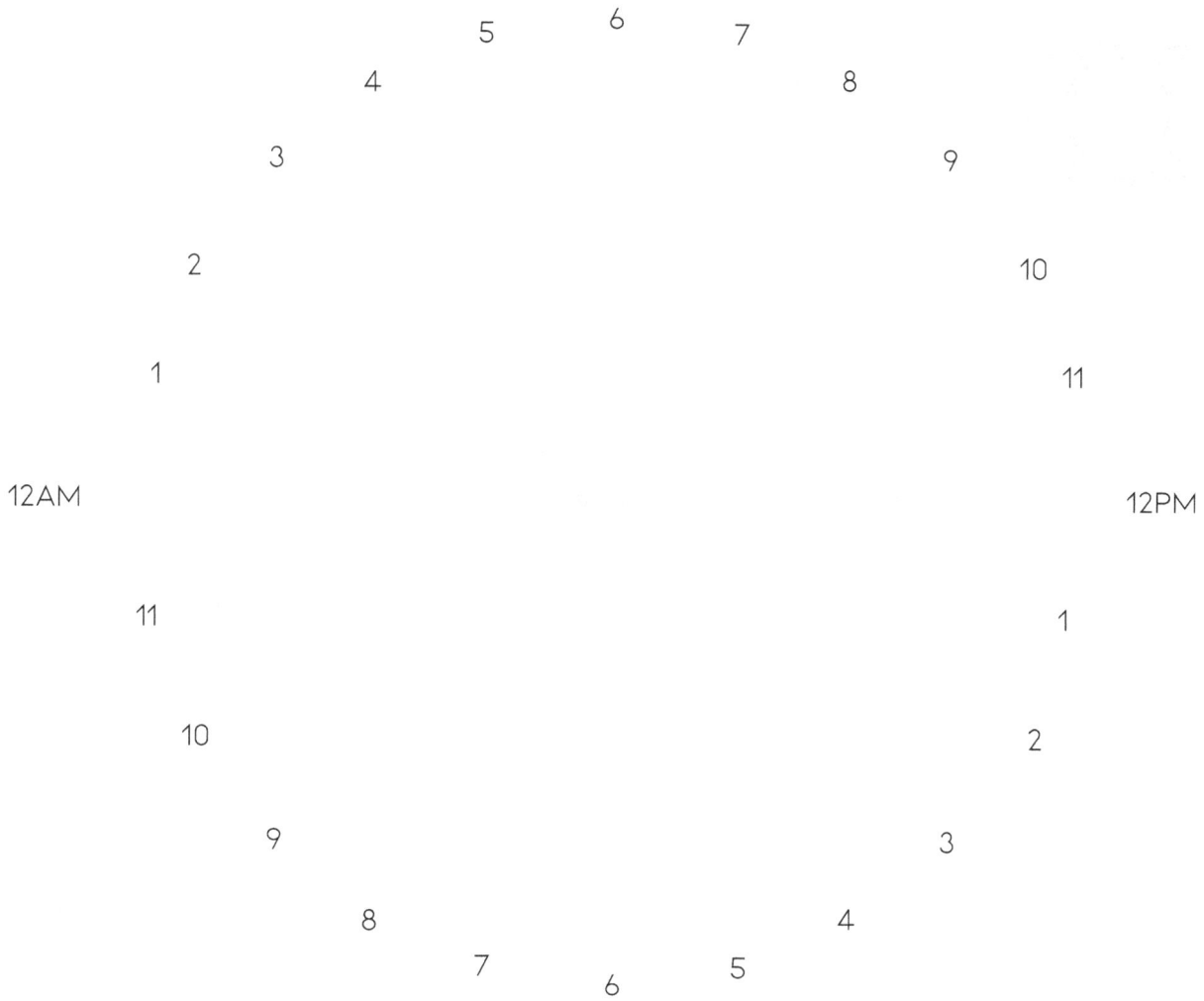

5   6   7
4   8
3   9
2   10
1   11

12AM   12PM

11   1
10   2
9   3
8   4
7   5
6

my WEEKLY SCHEDULE

THIS WEEK:

	Mon	Tue	Wed	Thur	Fri	Sat	Sun
7 am							
8 am							
9 am							
10 am							
11 am							
12 am							
1 pm							
2 pm							
3 pm							
4 pm							
5 pm							
6 pm							
7 pm							
8 pm							
9 pm							
10 pm							
11 pm							

my WEEKLY SCHEDULE

THIS WEEK:

	Sun	Mon	Tue	Wed	Thu	Fri	Sat
7 am							
8 am							
9 am							
10 am							
11 am							
12 am							
1 pm							
2 pm							
3 pm							
4 pm							
5 pm							
6 pm							
7 pm							
8 pm							
9 pm							
10 pm							
11 pm							

my MONTHLY PLAN

THE MONTH OF

GOAL #1

GOAL #2

GOAL #3

MOST IMPORTANT TASKS

NOTES & SCRIBBLES

Monday	*Tuesday*	*Wednesday*	*Thursday*	*Friday*	*Saturday*	*Sunday*

MONTHLY
– TOP GOALS –

MONTH OF:

TOP 5 MONTHLY GOALS

ACTION PLAN/STEPS

01

02

03

04

05

TOP GOALS: 1 2 3 4 5 6 7 8 9 10 11 12 13 14 15 16 17 18 19 20 21 22 23 24 25 26 27 28 29 30 31

NOTES:

PROJECT TIME TRACKER
– SPRINT SESSION TIMER –

DATE

1

TOTAL ALLOCATED
GOAL TIME

15 MIN TRACKER

*Check off every 15 minute
Sprint session you complete.*

2

TOTAL ALLOCATED
GOAL TIME

15 MIN TRACKER

*Check off every 15 minute
Sprint session you complete.*

3

TOTAL ALLOCATED
GOAL TIME

15 MIN TRACKER

*Check off every 15 minute
Sprint session you complete.*

PRIORITIZED GOALS & TIME TRACKER

TIME SPENT

TASK COMPLETED

NOTES

PROJECT MANAGER
- 5 WEEK GOAL TRACKER -

DATE _____

TOP 3 GOALS

ACTION PLAN

M	T	W	T	F	S	S

MONTH IN *review*

SUMMARIZE YOUR MONTH

TOP 3 ACCOMPLISHMENTS

01

02

03

NOTES & REFLECTION

MONTHLY HIGHLIGHTS

WHAT I CAN IMPROVE

NEXT MONTH FOCUS

WEEKLY *planner*

TOP WEEKLY GOALS

HOW I'M GOING TO ACCOMPLISH MY GOALS

01

02

03

URGENT

NOT URGENT

IMPORTANT

NOT IMPORTANT

WEEKLY *hour by hour*

	M	T	W	T	F	S	S
5 AM							
6 AM							
7 AM							
8 AM							
9 AM							
10 AM							
11 AM							
12 PM							
1 PM							
2 PM							
3 PM							
4 PM							
5 PM							
6 PM							
7 PM							
8 PM							
9 PM							
10 PM							

DAILY *goal tracker*

TOP PRIORITIES OF THE DAY

SECONDARY PRIORITIES

WISH LIST (NOT URGENT)

OTHER (IF I HAVE TIME)

NOTES

DAILY *schedule*

MY DAILY SCHEDULE

5 AM	2 PM
6 AM	3 PM
7 AM	4 PM
8 AM	5 PM
9 AM	6 PM
10 AM	7 PM
11 AM	8 PM
12 PM	9 PM
1 PM	10 PM

NOTES & REMINDERS

SCRIBBLES

DAILY *priorities*

M T W T F S S

MY TOP PRIORITIES OF THE DAY

01
02
03

TODAY'S TO-DO LIST

HOUR-BY-HOUR SCHEDULE

06
07
08
09
10
11
12
01
02
03
04
05
06
07
08
09
10

NOTES

REMINDERS

ACCOMPLISHMENTS

24-HOUR *planner*

TO DO LIST

DAILY SCHEDULE

0.00

1.00

2.00

3.00

4.00

5.00

6.00

DAILY MEAL PLANNER

7.00

BREAKFAST:

8.00

LUNCH:

9.00

DINNER:

10.00

SNACKS:

11.00

WATER:

12.00

NOTES

13.00

14.00

15.00

16.00

17.00

18.00

19.00

20.00

21.00

22.00

23.00

24.00

MONTHLY *Planner*

USE THE SPACE NEXT TO EACH DAY TO DOCUMENT PROGRESS AND OUTLINE GOALS.

NOTES & DOODLES

DAILY *schedule*

MY DAILY SCHEDULE

7 AM

8 AM

9 AM

10 AM

11 AM

12 PM

1 PM

2 PM

3 PM

4 PM

5 PM

6 PM

7 PM

8 PM

9 PM

10 PM

11 PM

12 PM

NOTES & REMINDERS

SCRIBBLES

Tracker

✦ 12-WEEK GOAL TRACKER ✦

USE THIS TRACKER TO DOCUMENT GOALS, SLEEP, WORKOUTS, HEALTHY EATING, HABIT CHANGES AND MORE.

FOCUS

GOAL TO RECORD

WEEK		DATE
START		
WK 01		
WK 02		
WK 03		
WK 04		
WK 05		
WK 06		
WK 07		
WK 08		
WK 09		
WK 10		
WK 11		
WK 12		
GOAL		
END		

HIGHS	LOWS	ACCOMPLISHMENTS

the WEEKLY AGENDA

	MON	TUES	WEDS	THURS	FRI	SAT	SUN
8AM							
9AM							
10AM							
11AM							
12PM							
1PM							
2PM							
3PM							
4PM							
5PM							
6PM							
7PM							
8PM							

My Monthly PLANNER

MONTH:

TOP
PRIORITY

TOP GOALS

MONDAY	TUESDAY	WEDNESDAY	THURSDAY	FRIDAY	SATURDAY	SUNDAY

NOTES:

My MONTHLY PLAN

THE MONTH OF

TOP 3 TASKS

MOST IMPORTANT TASKS

NOTES & SCRIBBLES

SUNDAY	MONDAY	TUESDAY	WEDNESDAY	THURSDAY	FRIDAY	SATURDAY

PROJECT PLANNER

Project:

Start Date:

Deadline:

Project Information & Action Plan

To Do

Notes & Reminders

Completed To Do List?

Note:

my PROJECT PLANNER

MY PROJECT GOALS

START

DUE

MY GOAL	ACTION PLAN	DUE ✓

TOOLS & RESOURCES

NOTES & DOODLES

my WORK HOURS LOG

TASK DETAILS

DATE   HOURS

TOTAL HOURS

my PROJECT PROGRESS

PROJECT ONE

Goal   *Start Date*   *Due Date*

PROJECT TWO

Goal   *Start Date*   *Due Date*

PROJECT THREE

Goal   *Start Date*   *Due Date*

PROJECT FOUR

Goal   *Start Date*   *Due Date*

PROJECT FIVE

Goal   *Start Date*   *Due Date*

PROJECT NAME:

ACTION STEPS / TASKS   DUE   ✓

my DAILY PRODUCTIVITY PLANNER

TODAY'S DATE

THE MAIN TASK

Daily Goals & Priorities

Start   *Finish*

SECONDARY TASKS

Notes & Reminders

1.

TODAY'S SCHEDULE

Start   *Finish*

2.

Daily Overview

Start   *Finish*

3.

Start   *Finish*

OTHER TASKS

NOTES & SCRIBBLES

1.

Start   *Finish*

2.

Start   *Finish*

3.

Start   *Finish*

my WEEKLY PLAN

MONDAY

TUESDAY

WEDNESDAY

THURSDAY

FRIDAY

SATURDAY

SUNDAY

TOP THREE TASKS

1.

2.

3.

OTHER TASKS

MY NOTES

PROJECT PLANNER

PROJECT TITLE: BUDGET:

START DATE: DUE DATE: DURATION: COMPLETED:

PROJECT TO DO LIST   IDEAS * DOODLES * CONCEPTS * NOTES

ACTION PLAN OVERVIEW

NOTES

my PRODUCTIVITY WHEEL

Jot down your daily activities, goals and priorities on the spaces below. Assign every activity a unique color by filling in the circle that corresponds with it. Color in each hour of the day based on which activity you have completed.

Are you utilizing your time effectively? Are you reaching goals and focusing your time on your most important priorities?

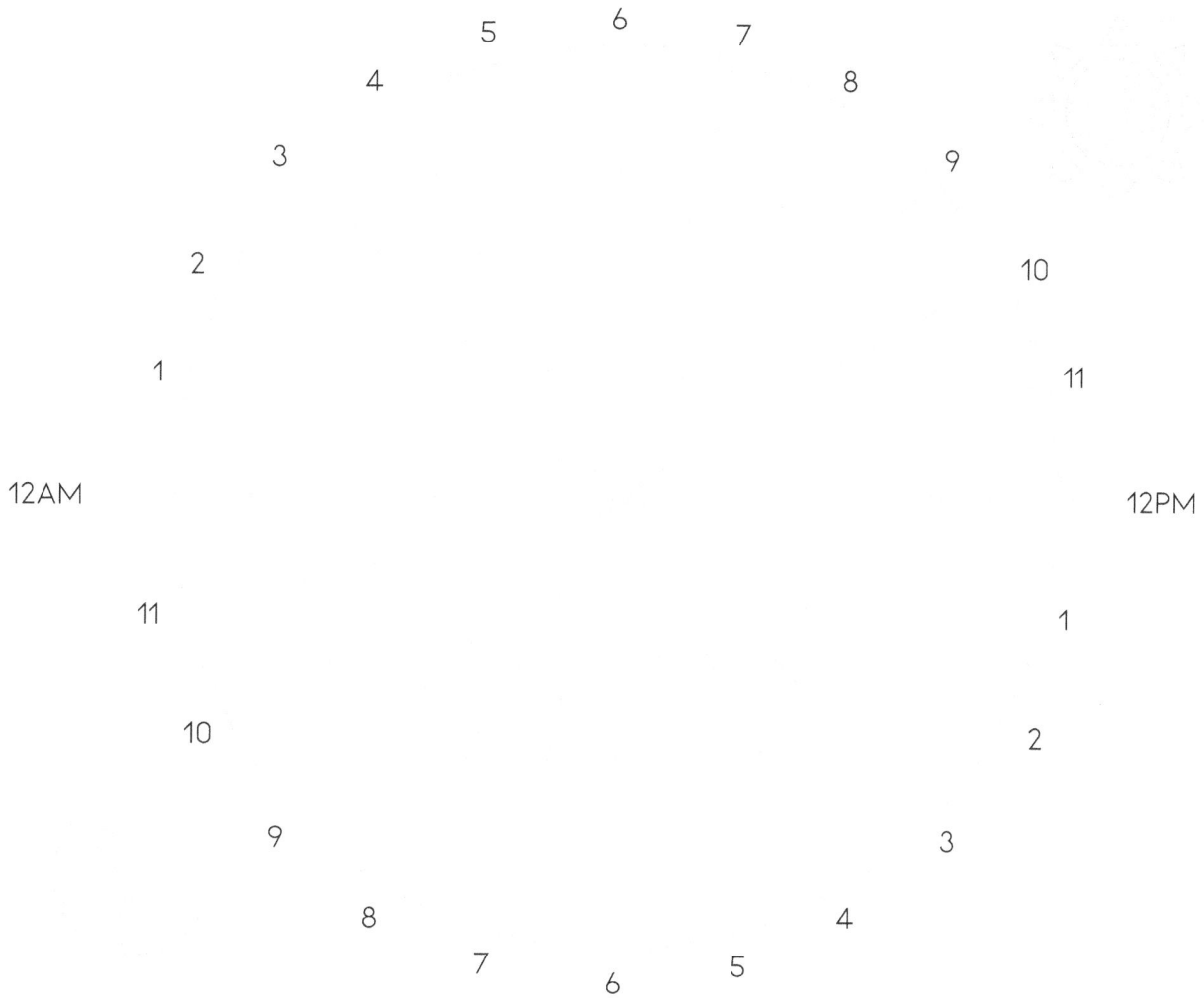

5   6   7

4   8

3   9

2   10

1   11

12AM   12PM

11   1

10   2

9   3

8   4

7   5

6

my WEEKLY SCHEDULE

THIS WEEK:

	Mon	Tue	Wed	Thur	Fri	Sat	Sun
7 am							
8 am							
9 am							
10 am							
11 am							
12 am							
1 pm							
2 pm							
3 pm							
4 pm							
5 pm							
6 pm							
7 pm							
8 pm							
9 pm							
10 pm							
11 pm							

my WEEKLY SCHEDULE

THIS WEEK:

	Sun	Mon	Tue	Wed	Thu	Fri	Sat
7 am							
8 am							
9 am							
10 am							
11 am							
12 am							
1 pm							
2 pm							
3 pm							
4 pm							
5 pm							
6 pm							
7 pm							
8 pm							
9 pm							
10 pm							
11 pm							

my MONTHLY PLAN

THE MONTH OF

GOAL #1

GOAL #2

GOAL #3

MOST IMPORTANT TASKS

NOTES & SCRIBBLES

Monday	*Tuesday*	*Wednesday*	*Thursday*	*Friday*	*Saturday*	*Sunday*

MONTHLY
– TOP GOALS –

MONTH OF:

TOP 5 MONTHLY GOALS

ACTION PLAN/STEPS

01

02

03

04

05

TOP GOALS: 1 2 3 4 5 6 7 8 9 10 11 12 13 14 15 16 17 18 19 20 21 22 23 24 25 26 27 28 29 30 31

NOTES:

PROJECT TIME TRACKER
– SPRINT SESSION TIMER –

DATE

1

TOTAL ALLOCATED
GOAL TIME

15 MIN TRACKER
*Check off every 15 minute
Sprint session you complete.*

2

TOTAL ALLOCATED
GOAL TIME

15 MIN TRACKER
*Check off every 15 minute
Sprint session you complete.*

3

TOTAL ALLOCATED
GOAL TIME

15 MIN TRACKER
*Check off every 15 minute
Sprint session you complete.*

PRIORITIZED GOALS & TIME TRACKER

TIME SPENT

TASK COMPLETED

NOTES

PROJECT MANAGER
- 5 WEEK GOAL TRACKER -

DATE

TOP 3 GOALS

ACTION PLAN

{

{

{

M	T	W	T	F	S	S

MONTH IN *review*

SUMMARIZE YOUR MONTH

TOP 3 ACCOMPLISHMENTS

01

02

03

NOTES & REFLECTION

MONTHLY HIGHLIGHTS   WHAT I CAN IMPROVE   NEXT MONTH FOCUS

WEEKLY *planner*

TOP WEEKLY GOALS

HOW I'M GOING TO ACCOMPLISH MY GOALS

01

02

03

URGENT

NOT URGENT

IMPORTANT

NOT IMPORTANT

WEEKLY *hour by hour*

	M	T	W	T	F	S	S
5 AM							
6 AM							
7 AM							
8 AM							
9 AM							
10 AM							
11 AM							
12 PM							
1 PM							
2 PM							
3 PM							
4 PM							
5 PM							
6 PM							
7 PM							
8 PM							
9 PM							
10 PM							

DAILY *goal tracker*

TOP PRIORITIES OF THE DAY

SECONDARY PRIORITIES

WISH LIST (NOT URGENT)

OTHER (IF I HAVE TIME)

NOTES

DAILY *schedule*

MY DAILY SCHEDULE

5 AM

6 AM

7 AM

8 AM

9 AM

10 AM

11 AM

12 PM

1 PM

2 PM

3 PM

4 PM

5 PM

6 PM

7 PM

8 PM

9 PM

10 PM

NOTES & REMINDERS

SCRIBBLES

DAILY *priorities*

DATE

M T W T F S S

MY TOP PRIORITIES OF THE DAY

01 _____

02 _____

03 _____

TODAY'S TO-DO LIST

HOUR-BY-HOUR SCHEDULE

06

07

08

09

10

11

12

01

02

03

04

05

06

07

08

09

10

NOTES   REMINDERS   ACCOMPLISHMENTS

24-HOUR *planner*

TO DO LIST

DAILY SCHEDULE

0.00

1.00

2.00

3.00

4.00

5.00

6.00

DAILY MEAL PLANNER   7.00

BREAKFAST: 8.00

LUNCH: 9.00

DINNER: 10.00

SNACKS: 11.00

WATER: 12.00

NOTES   13.00

14.00

15.00

16.00

17.00

18.00

19.00

20.00

21.00

22.00

23.00

24.00

MONTHLY *Planner*

USE THE SPACE NEXT TO EACH DAY TO DOCUMENT PROGRESS AND OUTLINE GOALS.

NOTES & DOODLES

DAILY *schedule*

MY DAILY SCHEDULE

7 AM	4 PM
8 AM	5 PM
9 AM	6 PM
10 AM	7 PM
11 AM	8 PM
12 PM	9 PM
1 PM	10 PM
2 PM	11 PM
3 PM	12 PM

NOTES & REMINDERS

SCRIBBLES

Tracker

✦ 12-WEEK GOAL TRACKER ✦

FOCUS

USE THIS TRACKER TO DOCUMENT GOALS, SLEEP, WORKOUTS, HEALTHY EATING, HABIT CHANGES AND MORE.

GOAL TO RECORD

WEEK		DATE
START		
WK 01		
WK 02		
WK 03		
WK 04		
WK 05		
WK 06		
WK 07		
WK 08		
WK 09		
WK 10		
WK 11		
WK 12		
GOAL		
END		

HIGHS	LOWS	ACCOMPLISHMENTS

the WEEKLY AGENDA

	MON	TUES	WEDS	THURS	FRI	SAT	SUN
8AM							
9AM							
10AM							
11AM							
12PM							
1PM							
2PM							
3PM							
4PM							
5PM							
6PM							
7PM							
8PM							

My Monthly PLANNER

MONTH:

**TOP
PRIORITY**

TOP GOALS

MONDAY	TUESDAY	WEDNESDAY	THURSDAY	FRIDAY	SATURDAY	SUNDAY

NOTES:

My MONTHLY PLAN

THE MONTH OF

TOP 3 TASKS

MOST IMPORTANT TASKS

NOTES & SCRIBBLES

SUNDAY	MONDAY	TUESDAY	WEDNESDAY	THURSDAY	FRIDAY	SATURDAY

PROJECT PLANNER

Project Information & Action Plan

Project:

Start Date:

Deadline:

To Do

Notes & Reminders

Completed To Do List?

Note:

my PROJECT PLANNER

MY PROJECT GOALS

MY GOAL　　　　　　ACTION PLAN　　　　DUE　✓

START

DUE

TOOLS & RESOURCES

NOTES & DOODLES

my WORK HOURS LOG

TASK DETAILS	DATE	HOURS

	TOTAL HOURS	

my PROJECT PROGRESS

PROJECT ONE

Goal   *Start Date*   *Due Date*

PROJECT TWO

Goal   *Start Date*   *Due Date*

PROJECT THREE

Goal   *Start Date*   *Due Date*

PROJECT FOUR

Goal   *Start Date*   *Due Date*

PROJECT FIVE

Goal   *Start Date*   *Due Date*

PROJECT NAME:

ACTION STEPS / TASKS	DUE	✓

my DAILY PRODUCTIVITY PLANNER

TODAY'S DATE

THE MAIN TASK

Daily Goals & Priorities

Start   *Finish*

SECONDARY TASKS

Notes & Reminders

1.

TODAY'S SCHEDULE

Start   *Finish*

2.

Daily Overview

Start   *Finish*

3.

Start   *Finish*

OTHER TASKS

NOTES & SCRIBBLES

1.

Start   *Finish*

2.

Start   *Finish*

3.

Start   *Finish*

my WEEKLY PLAN

MONDAY

TUESDAY

WEDNESDAY

THURSDAY

FRIDAY

SATURDAY

SUNDAY

THE WEEK OF

TOP THREE TASKS

1.

2.

3.

OTHER TASKS

MY NOTES

PROJECT PLANNER

PROJECT TITLE: BUDGET:

START DATE: DUE DATE: DURATION: COMPLETED:

PROJECT TO DO LIST   IDEAS * DOODLES * CONCEPTS * NOTES

ACTION PLAN OVERVIEW

NOTES

my PRODUCTIVITY WHEEL

Jot down your daily activities, goals and priorities on the spaces below. Assign every activity a unique color by filling in the circle that corresponds with it. Color in each hour of the day based on which activity you have completed.

Are you utilizing your time effectively? Are you reaching goals and focusing your time on your most important priorities?

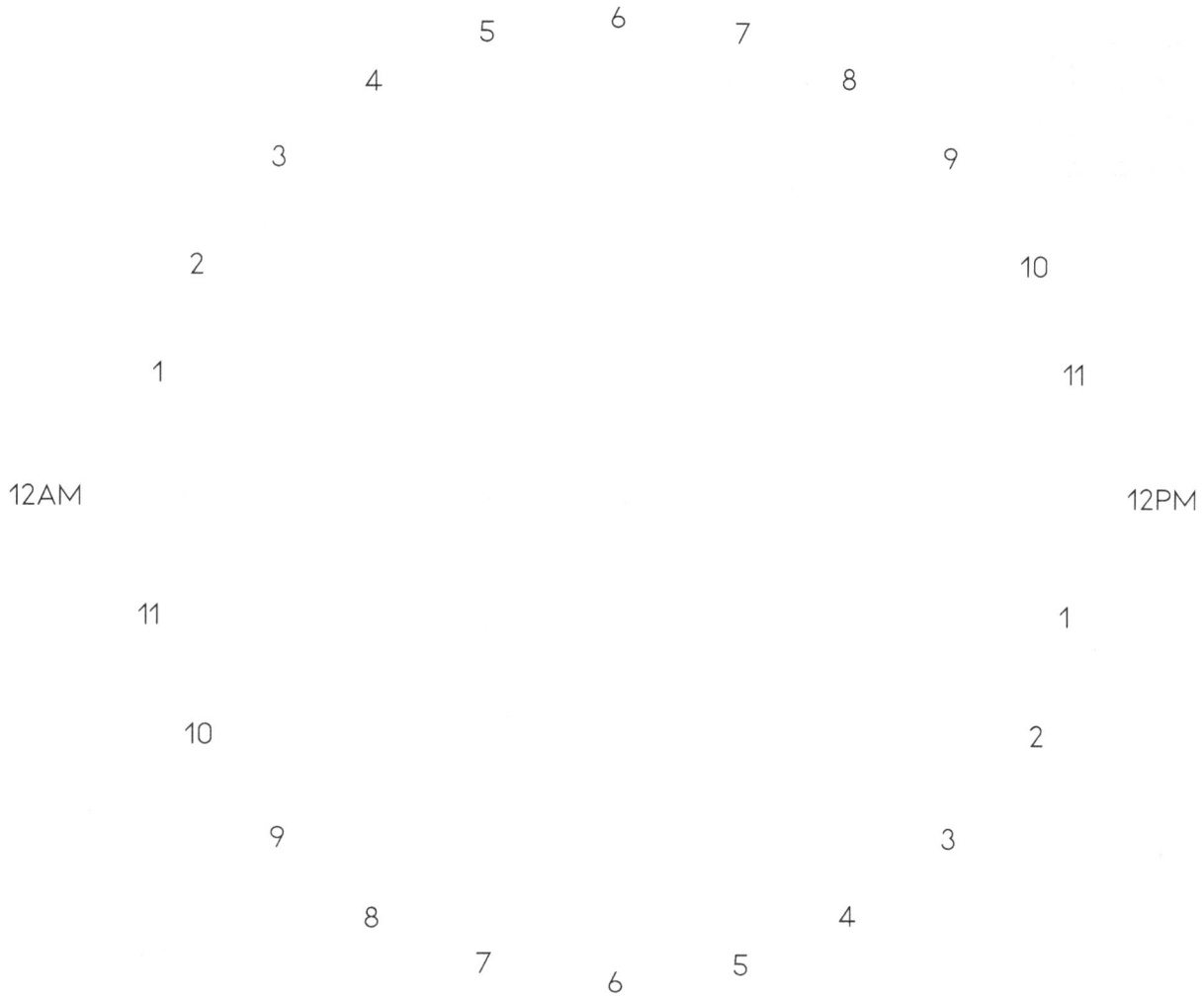

5   6   7

4   8

3   9

2   10

1   11

12AM   12PM

11   1

10   2

9   3

8   4

7   6   5

my WEEKLY SCHEDULE

THIS WEEK:

	Mon	Tue	Wed	Thur	Fri	Sat	Sun
7 am							
8 am							
9 am							
10 am							
11 am							
12 am							
1 pm							
2 pm							
3 pm							
4 pm							
5 pm							
6 pm							
7 pm							
8 pm							
9 pm							
10 pm							
11 pm							

my WEEKLY SCHEDULE

THIS WEEK:

	Sun	Mon	Tue	Wed	Thu	Fri	Sat
7 am							
8 am							
9 am							
10 am							
11 am							
12 am							
1 pm							
2 pm							
3 pm							
4 pm							
5 pm							
6 pm							
7 pm							
8 pm							
9 pm							
10 pm							
11 pm							

my MONTHLY PLAN

THE MONTH OF

GOAL #1   ## GOAL #2   ## GOAL #3

MOST IMPORTANT TASKS   NOTES & SCRIBBLES

Monday   *Tuesday*   *Wednesday*   *Thursday*   *Friday*   *Saturday*   *Sunday*

MONTHLY
– TOP GOALS –

MONTH OF:

TOP 5 MONTHLY GOALS

ACTION PLAN/STEPS

01

02

03

04

05

TOP GOALS: 1 2 3 4 5 6 7 8 9 10 11 12 13 14 15 16 17 18 19 20 21 22 23 24 25 26 27 28 29 30 31

NOTES:

PROJECT TIME TRACKER
– SPRINT SESSION TIMER –

DATE

1

TOTAL ALLOCATED
GOAL TIME

15 MIN TRACKER
*Check off every 15 minute
Sprint session you complete.*

2

TOTAL ALLOCATED
GOAL TIME

15 MIN TRACKER
*Check off every 15 minute
Sprint session you complete.*

3

TOTAL ALLOCATED
GOAL TIME

15 MIN TRACKER
*Check off every 15 minute
Sprint session you complete.*

PRIORITIZED GOALS & TIME TRACKER

TIME SPENT   TASK COMPLETED

NOTES

PROJECT MANAGER
- 5 WEEK GOAL TRACKER -

DATE

TOP 3 GOALS

ACTION PLAN

{

{

{

M	T	W	T	F	S	S

MONTH IN *review*

SUMMARIZE YOUR MONTH

TOP 3 ACCOMPLISHMENTS

01

02

03

NOTES & REFLECTION

MONTHLY HIGHLIGHTS

WHAT I CAN IMPROVE

NEXT MONTH FOCUS

WEEKLY *planner*

WEEK OF:

TOP WEEKLY GOALS

HOW I'M GOING TO ACCOMPLISH MY GOALS

01

02

03

URGENT

NOT URGENT

IMPORTANT

NOT IMPORTANT

WEEKLY *hour by hour*

	M	T	W	T	F	S	S
5 AM							
6 AM							
7 AM							
8 AM							
9 AM							
10 AM							
11 AM							
12 PM							
1 PM							
2 PM							
3 PM							
4 PM							
5 PM							
6 PM							
7 PM							
8 PM							
9 PM							
10 PM							

DAILY *goal tracker*

DATE:

TOP PRIORITIES OF THE DAY

SECONDARY PRIORITIES

WISH LIST (NOT URGENT)

OTHER (IF I HAVE TIME)

NOTES

DAILY *schedule*

MY DAILY SCHEDULE

5 AM	2 PM
6 AM	3 PM
7 AM	4 PM
8 AM	5 PM
9 AM	6 PM
10 AM	7 PM
11 AM	8 PM
12 PM	9 PM
1 PM	10 PM

NOTES & REMINDERS

SCRIBBLES

DAILY *priorities*

DATE

M T W T F S S

MY TOP PRIORITIES OF THE DAY

01

02

03

TODAY'S TO-DO LIST

HOUR-BY-HOUR SCHEDULE

06

07

08

09

10

11

12

01

02

03

04

05

06

07

08

09

10

NOTES   REMINDERS   ACCOMPLISHMENTS

24-HOUR *planner*

TO DO LIST

DAILY SCHEDULE

	0.00
	1.00
	2.00
	3.00
	4.00
	5.00
	6.00

DAILY MEAL PLANNER

7.00

BREAKFAST: 8.00

LUNCH: 9.00

DINNER: 10.00

SNACKS: 11.00

WATER: 12.00

NOTES

13.00

14.00

15.00

16.00

17.00

18.00

19.00

20.00

21.00

22.00

23.00

24.00

MONTHLY *Planner*

USE THE SPACE NEXT TO EACH DAY TO DOCUMENT PROGRESS AND OUTLINE GOALS.

NOTES & DOODLES

DAILY *schedule*

M T W T F S S

MY DAILY SCHEDULE

7 AM	4 PM
8 AM	5 PM
9 AM	6 PM
10 AM	7 PM
11 AM	8 PM
12 PM	9 PM
1 PM	10 PM
2 PM	11 PM
3 PM	12 PM

NOTES & REMINDERS

SCRIBBLES

Tracker

+ 12-WEEK GOAL TRACKER +

FOCUS

USE THIS TRACKER TO DOCUMENT GOALS, SLEEP, WORKOUTS, HEALTHY EATING, HABIT CHANGES AND MORE.

GOAL TO RECORD

WEEK		DATE
START		
WK 01		
WK 02		
WK 03		
WK 04		
WK 05		
WK 06		
WK 07		
WK 08		
WK 09		
WK 10		
WK 11		
WK 12		
GOAL		
END		

HIGHS	LOWS	ACCOMPLISHMENTS

the WEEKLY AGENDA

	MON	TUES	WEDS	THURS	FRI	SAT	SUN
8AM							
9AM							
10AM							
11AM							
12PM							
1PM							
2PM							
3PM							
4PM							
5PM							
6PM							
7PM							
8PM							

My Monthly PLANNER

MONTH:

TOP
PRIORITY

TOP GOALS

MONDAY	TUESDAY	WEDNESDAY	THURSDAY	FRIDAY	SATURDAY	SUNDAY

NOTES:

My MONTHLY PLAN

THE MONTH OF

TOP 3 TASKS

MOST IMPORTANT TASKS

NOTES & SCRIBBLES

SUNDAY	MONDAY	TUESDAY	WEDNESDAY	THURSDAY	FRIDAY	SATURDAY

PROJECT PLANNER

Project Information & Action Plan

Project:

Start Date:

Deadline:

To Do

Notes & Reminders

Completed To Do List?

Note:

my PROJECT PLANNER

MY PROJECT GOALS | MY GOAL | ACTION PLAN | DUE ✓

START

DUE

TOOLS & RESOURCES

NOTES & DOODLES

my WORK HOURS LOG

DATE   HOURS

TOTAL HOURS

my PROJECT PROGRESS

PROJECT ONE

Goal   *Start Date*   *Due Date*

PROJECT TWO

Goal   *Start Date*   *Due Date*

PROJECT THREE

Goal   *Start Date*   *Due Date*

PROJECT FOUR

Goal   *Start Date*   *Due Date*

PROJECT FIVE

Goal   *Start Date*   *Due Date*

PROJECT NAME:

ACTION STEPS / TASKS	DUE	✓

my DAILY PRODUCTIVITY PLANNER

TODAY'S DATE

THE MAIN TASK

Daily Goals & Priorities

Start   *Finish*

SECONDARY TASKS

Notes & Reminders

1.

TODAY'S SCHEDULE

Start   *Finish*

2.

Daily Overview

Start   *Finish*

3.

Start   *Finish*

OTHER TASKS

NOTES & SCRIBBLES

1.

Start   *Finish*

2.

Start   *Finish*

3.

Start   *Finish*

my WEEKLY PLAN

MONDAY

TUESDAY

WEDNESDAY

THURSDAY

FRIDAY

SATURDAY

SUNDAY

THE WEEK OF

TOP THREE TASKS

1.

2.

3.

OTHER TASKS

MY NOTES

PROJECT PLANNER

PROJECT TITLE: BUDGET:

START DATE: DUE DATE: DURATION: COMPLETED:

PROJECT TO DO LIST   IDEAS * DOODLES * CONCEPTS * NOTES

ACTION PLAN OVERVIEW

NOTES

my PRODUCTIVITY WHEEL

Jot down your daily activities, goals and priorities on the spaces below. Assign every activity a unique color by filling in the circle that corresponds with it. Color in each hour of the day based on which activity you have completed.

Are you utilizing your time effectively? Are you reaching goals and focusing your time on your most important priorities?

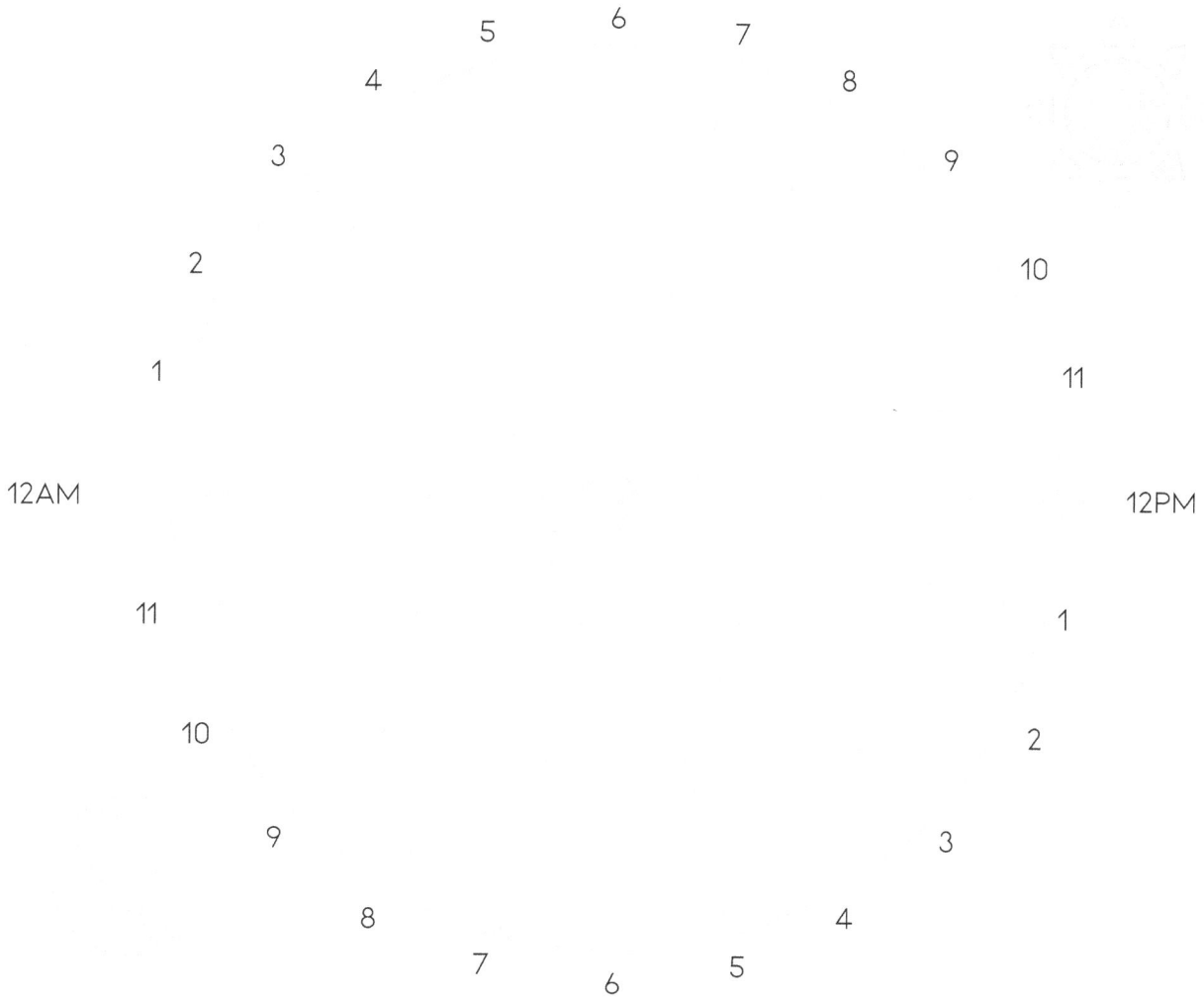

5   6   7

4   8

3   9

2   10

1   11

12AM   12PM

11   1

10   2

9   3

8   4

7   6   5

my WEEKLY SCHEDULE

THIS WEEK:

	Mon	Tue	Wed	Thur	Fri	Sat	Sun
7 am							
8 am							
9 am							
10 am							
11 am							
12 am							
1 pm							
2 pm							
3 pm							
4 pm							
5 pm							
6 pm							
7 pm							
8 pm							
9 pm							
10 pm							
11 pm							

my WEEKLY SCHEDULE

THIS WEEK:

	Sun	Mon	Tue	Wed	Thu	Fri	Sat
7 am							
8 am							
9 am							
10 am							
11 am							
12 am							
1 pm							
2 pm							
3 pm							
4 pm							
5 pm							
6 pm							
7 pm							
8 pm							
9 pm							
10 pm							
11 pm							

my MONTHLY PLAN

THE MONTH OF

GOAL #1   GOAL #2   GOAL #3

MOST IMPORTANT TASKS   NOTES & SCRIBBLES

Monday   *Tuesday*   *Wednesday*   *Thursday*   *Friday*   *Saturday*   *Sunday*

MONTHLY
- TOP GOALS -

MONTH OF:

TOP 5 MONTHLY GOALS

ACTION PLAN/STEPS

01

02

03

04

05

TOP GOALS: 1 2 3 4 5 6 7 8 9 10 11 12 13 14 15 16 17 18 19 20 21 22 23 24 25 26 27 28 29 30 31

NOTES:

PROJECT TIME TRACKER
– SPRINT SESSION TIMER –

DATE

1

TOTAL ALLOCATED
GOAL TIME

15 MIN TRACKER
*Check off every 15 minute
Sprint session you complete.*

2

TOTAL ALLOCATED
GOAL TIME

15 MIN TRACKER
*Check off every 15 minute
Sprint session you complete.*

3

TOTAL ALLOCATED
GOAL TIME

15 MIN TRACKER
*Check off every 15 minute
Sprint session you complete.*

PRIORITIZED GOALS & TIME TRACKER

TIME SPENT   TASK COMPLETED

NOTES

PROJECT MANAGER
- 5 WEEK GOAL TRACKER -

DATE

TOP 3 GOALS

ACTION PLAN

{

{

{

M	T	W	T	F	S	S

MONTH IN *review*

SUMMARIZE YOUR MONTH

TOP 3 ACCOMPLISHMENTS

01

02

03

NOTES & REFLECTION

MONTHLY HIGHLIGHTS

WHAT I CAN IMPROVE

NEXT MONTH FOCUS

WEEKLY *planner*

WEEK OF:

TOP WEEKLY GOALS

HOW I'M GOING TO ACCOMPLISH MY GOALS

01

02

03

URGENT

NOT URGENT

IMPORTANT

NOT IMPORTANT

WEEKLY *hour by hour*

	M	T	W	T	F	S	S
5 AM							
6 AM							
7 AM							
8 AM							
9 AM							
10 AM							
11 AM							
12 PM							
1 PM							
2 PM							
3 PM							
4 PM							
5 PM							
6 PM							
7 PM							
8 PM							
9 PM							
10 PM							

DAILY *goal tracker*

DATE:

TOP PRIORITIES OF THE DAY

SECONDARY PRIORITIES

WISH LIST (NOT URGENT)

OTHER (IF I HAVE TIME)

NOTES

DAILY *schedule*

MY DAILY SCHEDULE

5 AM	2 PM
6 AM	3 PM
7 AM	4 PM
8 AM	5 PM
9 AM	6 PM
10 AM	7 PM
11 AM	8 PM
12 PM	9 PM
1 PM	10 PM

NOTES & REMINDERS

SCRIBBLES

DAILY *priorities*

M T W T F S S

MY TOP PRIORITIES OF THE DAY

01
02
03

TODAY'S TO-DO LIST

HOUR-BY-HOUR SCHEDULE

06
07
08
09
10
11
12
01
02
03
04
05
06
07
08
09
10

NOTES	REMINDERS	ACCOMPLISHMENTS

24-HOUR *planner*

TO DO LIST

☐
☐
☐
☐
☐
☐
☐

DAILY MEAL PLANNER

BREAKFAST:

LUNCH:

DINNER:

SNACKS:

WATER: ○ ○ ○ ○ ○ ○ ○ ○

NOTES

DAILY SCHEDULE

0.00

1.00

2.00

3.00

4.00

5.00

6.00

7.00

8.00

9.00

10.00

11.00

12.00

13.00

14.00

15.00

16.00

17.00

18.00

19.00

20.00

21.00

22.00

23.00

24.00

MONTHLY *Planner*

USE THE SPACE NEXT TO EACH DAY TO DOCUMENT PROGRESS AND OUTLINE GOALS.

NOTES & DOODLES

DAILY *schedule*

MY DAILY SCHEDULE

7 AM	4 PM
8 AM	5 PM
9 AM	6 PM
10 AM	7 PM
11 AM	8 PM
12 PM	9 PM
1 PM	10 PM
2 PM	11 PM
3 PM	12 PM

NOTES & REMINDERS

SCRIBBLES

Tracker

✦ 12-WEEK GOAL TRACKER ✦

FOCUS

USE THIS TRACKER TO DOCUMENT GOALS, SLEEP, WORKOUTS, HEALTHY EATING, HABIT CHANGES AND MORE.

GOAL TO RECORD

WEEK		DATE
START		
WK 01		
WK 02		
WK 03		
WK 04		
WK 05		
WK 06		
WK 07		
WK 08		
WK 09		
WK 10		
WK 11		
WK 12		
GOAL		
END		

HIGHS	LOWS	ACCOMPLISHMENTS

the WEEKLY AGENDA

	MON	TUES	WEDS	THURS	FRI	SAT	SUN
8AM							
9AM							
10AM							
11AM							
12PM							
1PM							
2PM							
3PM							
4PM							
5PM							
6PM							
7PM							
8PM							

My Monthly PLANNER

MONTH:

TOP PRIORITY

TOP GOALS

MONDAY	TUESDAY	WEDNESDAY	THURSDAY	FRIDAY	SATURDAY	SUNDAY

NOTES:

My MONTHLY PLAN

THE MONTH OF

TOP 3 TASKS

MOST IMPORTANT TASKS

NOTES & SCRIBBLES

SUNDAY	MONDAY	TUESDAY	WEDNESDAY	THURSDAY	FRIDAY	SATURDAY

PROJECT PLANNER

Project Information & Action Plan

Project:

Start Date:

Deadline:

To Do

Notes & Reminders

Completed To Do List?

Note:

my PROJECT PLANNER

MY PROJECT GOALS   MY GOAL   ACTION PLAN   DUE ✓

START

DUE

TOOLS & RESOURCES

NOTES & DOODLES

my WORK HOURS LOG

TASK DETAILS	DATE	HOURS

TOTAL HOURS [   ]

my PROJECT PROGRESS

PROJECT ONE

Goal   *Start Date*   *Due Date*

PROJECT TWO

Goal   *Start Date*   *Due Date*

PROJECT THREE

Goal   *Start Date*   *Due Date*

PROJECT FOUR

Goal   *Start Date*   *Due Date*

PROJECT FIVE

Goal   *Start Date*   *Due Date*

PROJECT NAME:

ACTION STEPS / TASKS	DUE	✓

my DAILY PRODUCTIVITY PLANNER

TODAY'S DATE

THE MAIN TASK

Daily Goals & Priorities

Start   *Finish*

SECONDARY TASKS

Notes & Reminders

1.

TODAY'S SCHEDULE

Start   *Finish*

2.

Daily Overview

Start   *Finish*

3.

Start   *Finish*

OTHER TASKS

NOTES & SCRIBBLES

1.

Start   *Finish*

2.

Start   *Finish*

3.

Start   *Finish*

my WEEKLY PLAN

MONDAY

TUESDAY

WEDNESDAY

THURSDAY

FRIDAY

SATURDAY

SUNDAY

THE WEEK OF

TOP THREE TASKS

1.

2.

3.

OTHER TASKS

MY NOTES

PROJECT PLANNER

PROJECT TITLE: BUDGET:

START DATE: DUE DATE: DURATION: COMPLETED:

PROJECT TO DO LIST   IDEAS * DOODLES * CONCEPTS * NOTES

ACTION PLAN OVERVIEW

NOTES

my PRODUCTIVITY WHEEL

Jot down your daily activities, goals and priorities on the spaces below. Assign every activity a unique color by filling in the circle that corresponds with it. Color in each hour of the day based on which activity you have completed.

Are you utilizing your time effectively? Are you reaching goals and focusing your time on your most important priorities?

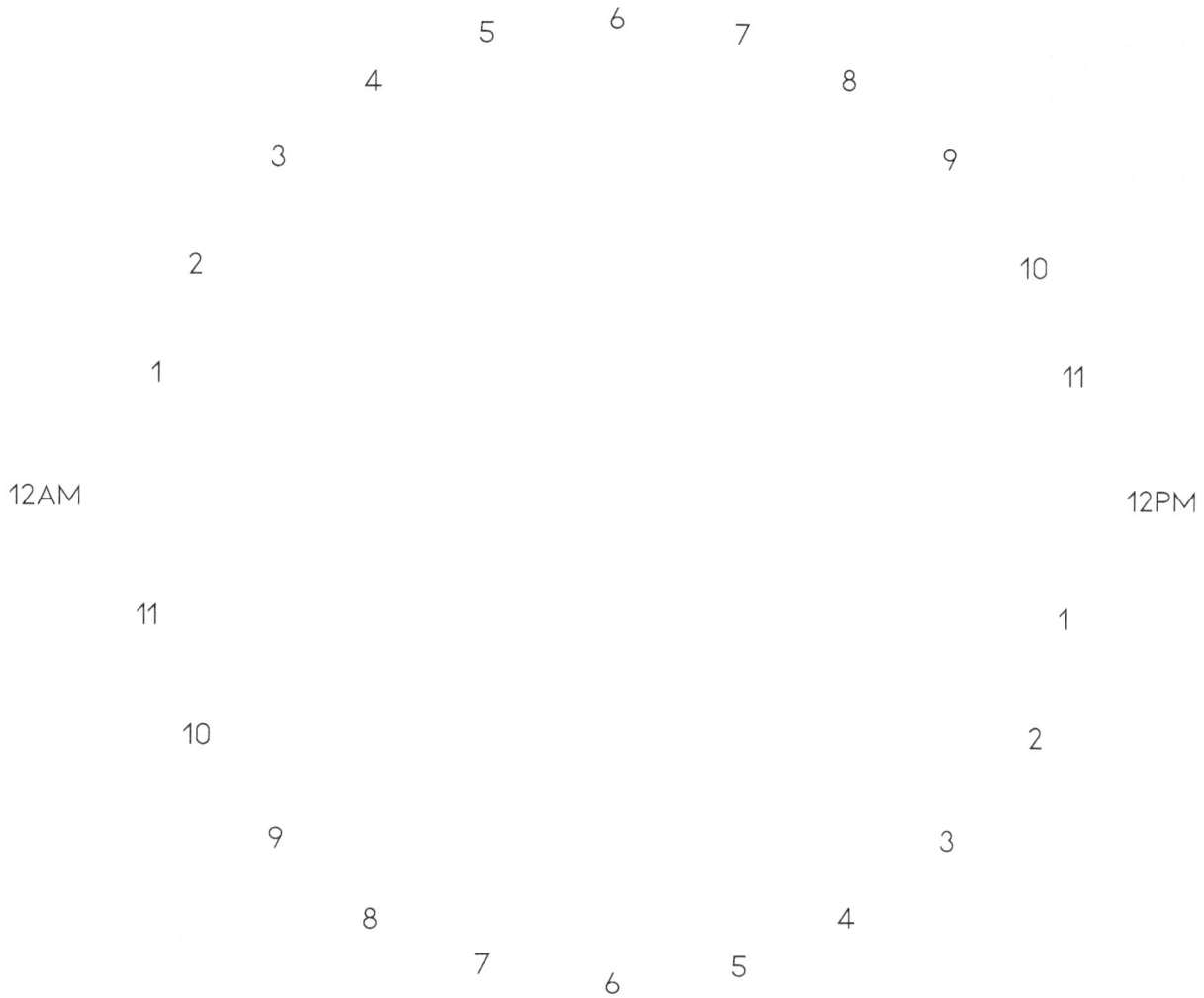

5   6   7

4   8

3   9

2   10

1   11

12AM   12PM

11   1

10   2

9   3

8   4

7   6   5

my WEEKLY SCHEDULE

THIS WEEK:

	Mon	Tue	Wed	Thur	Fri	Sat	Sun
7 am							
8 am							
9 am							
10 am							
11 am							
12 am							
1 pm							
2 pm							
3 pm							
4 pm							
5 pm							
6 pm							
7 pm							
8 pm							
9 pm							
10 pm							
11 pm							

my WEEKLY SCHEDULE

THIS WEEK:

	Sun	Mon	Tue	Wed	Thu	Fri	Sat
7 am							
8 am							
9 am							
10 am							
11 am							
12 am							
1 pm							
2 pm							
3 pm							
4 pm							
5 pm							
6 pm							
7 pm							
8 pm							
9 pm							
10 pm							
11 pm							

my MONTHLY PLAN

THE MONTH OF

GOAL #1   **GOAL #2**   **GOAL #3**

MOST IMPORTANT TASKS   NOTES & SCRIBBLES

Monday   *Tuesday*   *Wednesday*   *Thursday*   *Friday*   *Saturday*   *Sunday*

MONTHLY
– TOP GOALS –

MONTH OF:

TOP 5 MONTHLY GOALS

01

02

03

04

05

ACTION PLAN/STEPS

TOP GOALS: 1 2 3 4 5 6 7 8 9 10 11 12 13 14 15 16 17 18 19 20 21 22 23 24 25 26 27 28 29 30 31

NOTES:

PROJECT TIME TRACKER
– SPRINT SESSION TIMER –

DATE

1

TOTAL ALLOCATED
GOAL TIME

15 MIN TRACKER

*Check off every 15 minute
Sprint session you complete.*

2

TOTAL ALLOCATED
GOAL TIME

15 MIN TRACKER

*Check off every 15 minute
Sprint session you complete.*

3

TOTAL ALLOCATED
GOAL TIME

15 MIN TRACKER

*Check off every 15 minute
Sprint session you complete.*

PRIORITIZED GOALS & TIME TRACKER

TIME SPENT

TASK COMPLETED

NOTES

PROJECT MANAGER
- 5 WEEK GOAL TRACKER -

DATE ....

TOP 3 GOALS

ACTION PLAN

{ ☐ ....
☐ ....
☐ ....

{ ☐ ....
☐ ....
☐ ....

{ ☐ ....
☐ ....
☐ ....

M	T	W	T	F	S	S

MONTH IN *review*

SUMMARIZE YOUR MONTH

TOP 3 ACCOMPLISHMENTS

NOTES & REFLECTION

01

02

03

MONTHLY HIGHLIGHTS

WHAT I CAN IMPROVE

NEXT MONTH FOCUS

WEEKLY *planner*

WEEK OF:

TOP WEEKLY GOALS

HOW I'M GOING TO ACCOMPLISH MY GOALS

01

02

03

URGENT

NOT URGENT

IMPORTANT

NOT IMPORTANT

WEEKLY *hour by hour*

	M	T	W	T	F	S	S
5 AM							
6 AM							
7 AM							
8 AM							
9 AM							
10 AM							
11 AM							
12 PM							
1 PM							
2 PM							
3 PM							
4 PM							
5 PM							
6 PM							
7 PM							
8 PM							
9 PM							
10 PM							

DAILY *goal tracker*

DATE:

TOP PRIORITIES OF THE DAY

SECONDARY PRIORITIES

WISH LIST (NOT URGENT)

OTHER (IF I HAVE TIME)

NOTES

DAILY *schedule*

MY DAILY SCHEDULE

5 AM	2 PM
6 AM	3 PM
7 AM	4 PM
8 AM	5 PM
9 AM	6 PM
10 AM	7 PM
11 AM	8 PM
12 PM	9 PM
1 PM	10 PM

NOTES & REMINDERS

SCRIBBLES

DAILY *priorities*

DATE

M T W T F S S

MY TOP PRIORITIES OF THE DAY

01

02

03

TODAY'S TO-DO LIST

HOUR-BY-HOUR SCHEDULE

06

07

08

09

10

11

12

01

02

03

04

05

06

07

08

09

10

NOTES

REMINDERS

ACCOMPLISHMENTS

24-HOUR *planner*

TO DO LIST

DAILY SCHEDULE

0.00

1.00

2.00

3.00

4.00

5.00

6.00

DAILY MEAL PLANNER

7.00

BREAKFAST:

8.00

LUNCH:

9.00

DINNER:

10.00

SNACKS:

11.00

WATER:

12.00

NOTES

13.00

14.00

15.00

16.00

17.00

18.00

19.00

20.00

21.00

22.00

23.00

24.00

MONTHLY *Planner*

USE THE SPACE NEXT TO EACH DAY TO DOCUMENT PROGRESS AND OUTLINE GOALS.

NOTES & DOODLES

DAILY *schedule*

MY DAILY SCHEDULE

7 AM	4 PM
8 AM	5 PM
9 AM	6 PM
10 AM	7 PM
11 AM	8 PM
12 PM	9 PM
1 PM	10 PM
2 PM	11 PM
3 PM	12 PM

NOTES & REMINDERS

SCRIBBLES

Tracker

✦ 12-WEEK GOAL TRACKER ✦

FOCUS

USE THIS TRACKER TO DOCUMENT GOALS, SLEEP, WORKOUTS, HEALTHY EATING, HABIT CHANGES AND MORE.

GOAL TO RECORD

WEEK		DATE
START		
WK 01		
WK 02		
WK 03		
WK 04		
WK 05		
WK 06		
WK 07		
WK 08		
WK 09		
WK 10		
WK 11		
WK 12		
GOAL		
END		

HIGHS	LOWS	ACCOMPLISHMENTS

the WEEKLY AGENDA

	MON	TUES	WEDS	THURS	FRI	SAT	SUN
8AM							
9AM							
10AM							
11AM							
12PM							
1PM							
2PM							
3PM							
4PM							
5PM							
6PM							
7PM							
8PM							

My Monthly PLANNER

MONTH:

**TOP
PRIORITY**

TOP GOALS

MONDAY	TUESDAY	WEDNESDAY	THURSDAY	FRIDAY	SATURDAY	SUNDAY

NOTES:

My MONTHLY PLAN

THE MONTH OF

TOP 3 TASKS

MOST IMPORTANT TASKS

NOTES & SCRIBBLES

SUNDAY	MONDAY	TUESDAY	WEDNESDAY	THURSDAY	FRIDAY	SATURDAY

PROJECT PLANNER

Project:

Project Information & Action Plan

Start Date:

Deadline:

To Do

Notes & Reminders

Completed To Do List?

Note:

my PROJECT PLANNER

MY PROJECT GOALS

START

DUE

MY GOAL	ACTION PLAN	DUE	✓

TOOLS & RESOURCES

NOTES & DOODLES

my WORK HOURS LOG

TASK DETAILS

DATE   HOURS

TOTAL HOURS

my PROJECT PROGRESS

PROJECT ONE

Goal   *Start Date*   *Due Date*

PROJECT TWO

Goal   *Start Date*   *Due Date*

PROJECT THREE

Goal   *Start Date*   *Due Date*

PROJECT FOUR

Goal   *Start Date*   *Due Date*

PROJECT FIVE

Goal   *Start Date*   *Due Date*

PROJECT NAME:

ACTION STEPS / TASKS	DUE	✓

my DAILY PRODUCTIVITY PLANNER

TODAY'S DATE

THE MAIN TASK

Daily Goals & Priorities

Start   *Finish*

SECONDARY TASKS

Notes & Reminders

1.

TODAY'S SCHEDULE

Start   *Finish*

2.

Daily Overview

Start   *Finish*

3.

Start   *Finish*

OTHER TASKS

NOTES & SCRIBBLES

1.

Start   *Finish*

2.

Start   *Finish*

3.

Start   *Finish*

my WEEKLY PLAN

MONDAY

TUESDAY

WEDNESDAY

THURSDAY

FRIDAY

SATURDAY

SUNDAY

THE WEEK OF

TOP THREE TASKS

1.

2.

3.

OTHER TASKS

MY NOTES

PROJECT PLANNER

PROJECT TITLE: BUDGET:

START DATE: DUE DATE: DURATION: COMPLETED:

PROJECT TO DO LIST   IDEAS * DOODLES * CONCEPTS * NOTES

ACTION PLAN OVERVIEW

NOTES